Mobil New Ze,

Native Trees
of New Zealand 1

J. T. Salmon

REED

Front cover: A flower of the rewarewa, *Knightia excelsia*.
Title page: Flowers of the kowhai, *Sophora tetraptera*.

Published by Reed Books, a division of Reed Publishing (NZ) Ltd,
39 Rawene Road, Birkenhead, Auckland. Associated companies,
branches and representatives throughout the world.

First published 1998
Text © J. T. Salmon 1998
Photographs © J. T. Salmon 1998
Layout by Graeme Leather

ISBN 0 7900 0558 1

Printed in Singapore

Contents

Introduction

Native Trees of New Zealand 1 and *2* provide concise, portable guides to the identification of New Zealand's native trees. The text and photographs are based on my larger book, *The Trees in New Zealand: Native Trees*, although the number of photographs and species selected is, of course, much reduced. I refer readers to the larger book for a full introduction to New Zealand's forests and native trees.

The classification system used is based on *Flora of New Zealand* (Vol. 1, 1961, by H.H. Allan and Vol. 2, 1970, by L.B. Moore and E. Edgar). Common names and the Maori names for the trees, wherever they exist, are included with the botanical names. Technical terms are kept to a minimum, and those used are explained in the glossary.

When the first Europeans arrived in New Zealand they found a land clothed with dense, almost inpenetrable, luxuriant forests which extended from coastal regions to 600–900 metres altitude over much of the land. Most of this has now gone, cleared for pasture and settlement, but good examples still exist in forest parks, national parks and reserves dotted around the country. Known by the locals as 'the bush', these forests fall primarily into two forest types: (1) the conifer-hardwoods, dominated by either the podocarp trees or the kauri; (2) the beech forests dominated by the four species of trees belonging to the genus *Nothofagus*. These forests are mostly dense, intimate associations of species with only occasional pure stands of any one species. When they do occur such stands are usually small in area.

Typical North Island beech forest in the Kaimanawa Forest Park.

Rimu, matai and miro trees in podocarp-hardwood forest at Opepe Bush.

The dominant species of New Zealand forests have an ancestry which reaches back far into antiquity, and New Zealand podocarp forests contain more species with ancient lineages than similar forests elsewhere. Our beech trees have an ancestry as old as that of the podocarps, but both the podocarps and the beeches are surpassed by the kauris which first appeared during the Jurassic period of geological time, about 135–190 million years ago, in Gondwanaland. The Swedish botanist Florin suggests that the New Zealand kauri was living during the Permian period, 230 million years ago. Fossil remains of podocarps and beeches are found in deposits of the ancient Gondwanaland continent. In New Zealand glacial periods never completely exterminated all forests as happened in Northern Hemisphere lands. There always persisted refuges from which the land could be reforested.

The oldest living things in the world are trees, some species of which can reach an age of 5000 years. Kauri trees in New Zealand have been shown from growth rings to be over 2000 years old, while a tree felled at Mercury Bay could have been over 4000 years old. Podocarp species are known to live for 800 years and one tree felled near Taihape in 1906 was 435 years old.

Native Trees of New Zealand 1 and *2* aim to provide easy identification of the major species likely to be found by the bush walker or botanical enthusiast. I hope they contribute to readers' enjoyment and appreciation of our distinctive native trees.

J. T. Salmon

1 Kahikatea / White Pine
Dacrycarpus dacrydioides

Appearance
- Passes through several stages: seedling is straggly, juvenile form is conical; when mature crown opens, branches become stouter and more ascending.
- *Height:* up to 60 m; tallest in New Zealand.

- *Trunk:* up to 1.6 m through; sometimes buttressed.
- *Bark:* brown, white or grey horizontal bands when young, mature tree grey; smooth, scales off in large, ovoid flakes.

Foliage, Flowers & Fruit

- *Foliage:* juvenile, semi-adult and adult foliage may occur on same tree. Juvenile leaves 7 mm by 1 mm, slightly curved with sharply pointed tips; more or less in 2 rows along stems. Semi-adult leaves similar in shape but shorter, only up to 4 mm long, arranged more around the stems. Adult leaves up to 2 mm long, scale-like and closely appressed to stems.

- *Flowers:* Sept–Oct; male cones and female ovules borne on tips of branches on separate trees.
- *Fruit:* seeds ripen Apr/May, egg-shaped with bright orange-red receptacle.

Distribution & Habitat

- Widespread particularly in swampy areas, but also on dry sites and hillsides.
- Sea level to 600 m.

▼ Male cones with mature foliage. (approx x1)

▼ Ripe seeds on their red receptacles, April. (approx x1)

2 Matai / Black Pine
Prumnopitys taxifolia

Appearance

- Saplings have long, wiry, intertwining branches; mature tree has broad crown held on stout, erect, spreading branches.
- *Height:* up to 25 m.
- *Trunk:* up to 1.3 m through.
- *Bark:* grey-brown; hammer marked on mature trees, flakes off in thick rounded or ovoid chunks leaving reddish blotches.

Foliage, Flowers & Fruit

- *Foliage:* leaves dark blue-green above, silvery-blue below, darker with age; 1 cm long by 10–20 mm wide, straight or slightly curved; set wide apart in 2 rows; strong smell when crushed.
- *Flowers:* Oct–Nov, male and female flowers borne on separate trees.

- *Fruit:* ripens Nov–Mar after 15 months; globular deep blue-black seed, up to 9 mm across with pale purplish bloom.

Distribution & Habitat

- Throughout New Zealand in lowland forest.
- Sea level to 500 m.

▼ Mature foliage and ripe male cones, Nov. (approx x1)

▼ A ripe seed with its typical purplish bloom, Feb. (approx x1)

3 Miro / Brown Pine
Prumnopitys ferruginea

Appearance

- Juvenile tree has longer leaves and drooping habit; adult tall with rounded crown.
- *Height:* up to 25 m.
- *Trunk:* up to 1 m through.
- *Bark:* light greyish brown; finely hammer marked on mature trees, scaling off in thick flakes.

Foliage, Flowers & Fruit

- *Foliage:* leaves of juvenile light green or brownish red above, up to 3 cm long; adult dark green above, paler below; 15–20 mm long by 2–3 mm wide, with more rounded tips; lie in 2 rows on branchlets.
- *Flowers:* Sept–Oct; male and female borne on separate trees, singly at end of short axillary branchlet.
- *Fruit:* Sept–Nov after 12 months; reddish; male has solitary catkins; female, solitary at end of short stalk.

Distribution & Habitat

- Widespread in lowland forests.
- Sea level to 1000 m.

▲ Mature foliage and male cones, Oct.

◄ A cluster of ripe miro seeds, Nov. (slightly enlarged)

4 **Totara**
Podocarpus totara

Appearance

- In early stages spreading and bushy; mature tree open in habit, top tends to die back; enormous roots over ground.
- *Height:* up to 30 m.
- *Trunk:* up to 2 m through.
- *Bark:* reddish brown; thick, stringy and usually deeply furrowed.

Foliage, Flowers & Fruit

- *Foliage:* stiff prickly leaves are mid-green above, paler below; 1.3–3 cm long by 3–4 mm wide; sessile (no stalk); juvenile browner, narrower (1–2 mm wide).
- *Flowers:* Nov–Dec; male, female cones borne on separate trees; singly or clusters of 2–5 on single peduncle.
- *Fruit:* Mar–May; green seed set on red, berry-like receptacle.

Distribution & Habitat

- Widespread, found together in lowland forests.
- Sea level to 600 m.

▼ Mature foliage and ripe seeds in their receptacles, April. (approx x1)

▼ Bark of totara.

◀ The Pouakani totara near Mangapehi, 1979.

Silver pine
Monoao colensoi

Appearance
- Cone-shaped when young; mature tree has moderately spreading crown.
- *Height:* up to 15 m.
- *Trunk:* up to 1 m through; usually straight, clear of branches for some distance.
- *Bark:* silver-grey brown. Juvenile: irregular longitudinal ridging and pimpling. Mature: thicker, peeling in chunky layers.

Family PODOCARPACEAE
Genus *Monoao*

Foliage, Flowers & Fruit

- *Foliage:* leaves of juvenile 12 mm long, narrow and pointed; semi-adult smaller, flattened, in 2 opposite rows; adult leaves 4–5 mm long, thick, keeled, scale-like, appressed to branches in 4 rows.
- *Flowers:* Sept–Nov; terminal. Male: 3–4 mm, small, solitary. Female: solitary or in pairs.

- *Fruit:* seeds ripen April; deep blue-black on cup-like base.

Distribution & Habitat

- From Mangonui in Northland to Mt Ruapehu; in South Is. along west coast in shady conditions.
- Sea level to 950 m.

▲ Ripe male cone, Oct. (x4)

▲ Ripe female cone, Apr. (x4)

▶ Adult leaves with irregularly arranged stomata visible. (x4)

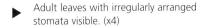

6 Rimu / Red Pine
Dacrydium cupressinum

Appearance

- The open-branched juvenile forms a pyramidal tree. Adult is very tall, straight-trunked with spreading crown and graceful, pendulous foliage.

- *Height:* 20–35 m, sometimes 60 m.
- *Trunk:* up to 1.5 m through.
- *Bark:* dark, greyish-brown; stringy, peeling in long, thick flakes.

Foliage, Flowers & Fruit

- *Foliage:* soft pliable juvenile leaves are olive green, may turn bronze in winter; juvenile 7 mm long by 1 mm wide, semi-adult up to 4 mm long, adult 2–3 mm long, elongated and keeled; as tree ages become more closely set and scale-like, overlapping around branchlets.

- *Flowers:* Sept–Jan; borne on separate trees; appear irregularly at tips of branchlets, usually solitary.
- *Fruit:* seeds ripen from Mar; dark, about 3 mm, on fleshy red base.

Distribution & Habitat

- Widespread in main islands.
- Sea level to 600 m.

▼ Adult foliage and male cones, Nov. (approx x1)

▼ Adult foliage and ripe seeds on their red receptacles, Apr. (x4)

7 Monoao
Halocarpus kirkii

Appearance

- Younger trees taper upwards, very graceful. Mature tree has tall trunk to spreading open-branched crown; similar appearance to small kauri.
- *Height:* up to 25 m.

- *Trunk:* up to 1 m through.
- *Bark:* juvenile: smooth, unflaking; mature: grey-brown, thick, pustular (blistered) texture, peels in irregular flakes.

Foliage, Flowers & Fruit

- *Foliage:* leathery juvenile leaves up to 4 cm long, 3 mm wide may persist on lower branches of trees to 10 m high; thick, scale-like adult leaves 2–3 mm long, overlapping and appressed to branchlets in 4 rows; irregularly arranged stomata.
- *Flowers:* Nov–Dec; cones borne on separate trees.

- *Fruit:* seeds ripen Apr after 18 months; black seed on orange base.

Distribution & Habitat

- Sporadically in lowland forests from Hokianga Harbour south to Coromandel Peninsula.
- Sea level to 700 m.

▲ Adult leaves have many irregularly arranged stomata. (x3)

◀ Juvenile leaves. (x1)

8 Tanekaha / Celery pine
Phyllocladus trichomanoides

Appearance
- A tall, pyramidal, upright-branched tree.
- *Height:* up to 20 m.
- *Trunk:* up to 1 m through.
- *Bark:* juvenile mottled greyish-green, mature reddish-brown; smooth.

Foliage, Flowers & Fruit

- *Foliage:* true leaves occur on seedlings, reddish brown, narrow, up to 2 cm long. Mature foliage deep green; phylloclades (up to 2.5 cm long) are stout, thick-stemmed, arranged in 2 rows on rachides (up to 30 cm long) arising in whorls from the branches. Each rachide has 9–15 phylloclades, giving appearance of a celery leaf.
- *Flowers:* Oct–Jan. Male cones crimson changing to deep purple, arise in terminal clusters at branch tips; female cones arise on margins of modified phylloclades.
- *Fruit:* seeds ripen about Apr; purplish; up to 3 mm long.

Distribution & Habitat

- Lowland forests from North Cape to Wanganui in North Is., Northern Marlborough and west Nelson in the South Is.
- Sea level to 800 m.

▼ Male cones at the tip of a rachide (branchlet) surrounded by a whorl of phylloclades, Oct. (x1.5)

▼ Whorls of rachides bearing phylloclades and female cones, Oct. (approx x1)

Toatoa
Phyllocladus toatoa

Appearance
- A tapering, roughly pyramidal, upright-branched tree.
- *Height:* up to 15 m.
- *Trunk:* up to 60 cm through.
- *Bark:* light brown with grey patches; coarse; can be heavily coated by lichens and mosses.

Foliage, Flowers & Fruit
- *Foliage:* juvenile phylloclades sea-green, mature bronzed; 4–6 cm long by 2–4 cm wide; wedge-shaped, thick and leathery, finely toothed margins.

- *Flowers:* Dec–Mar. Sexes may be separate on the same tree or on different trees. Male cones arise in clusters of 10–20 on thick stalks at tips of branchlets, female in terminal clusters on short stalks off central stem.
- *Fruit:* seeds ripen Jul; purple; 3 mm long, project from green bracts.

Distribution & Habitat
- From Mangonui south to Rotorua.
- Sea level to 600 m.

▼ Male cones, Dec. (approx x1)

▼ Phylloclades of toatoa with female cones along the rachides. (x0.5)

◀ A small tree of toatoa.

10 Kawaka and Pahautea
Libocedrus plumosa and *L. bidwillii*

Appearance
- Very similar in appearance, both cone-shaped with almost horizontally spreading, heavy branches.

- *Height:* Kawaka to 20 m; pahautea to 25 m.
- *Trunk:* to 1 m through, tapering.
- *Bark:* pinkish-tan; parchment-like, peels in long, narrow strips.

Foliage, Flowers & Fruit

- *Foliage:* juvenile leaves in both trees dull, blue-green, short (to 7 mm), broad, flattened and feathery. Kawaka adult leaves mostly compressed; branchlets have 4 rows of closely set leaves, each about 5 mm long. Pahautea adult: triangular, sharply pointed tips, appressed, each about 2 mm long.
- *Flowers:* very small; separate male and female on same tree. Kawaka cones (4–6 mm long) appear Sept–Oct, singly at tips of branchlets. Pahautea cones more prolific, arise in same way as kawaka and very similar in appearance but longer (6–11 mm).
- *Fruit:* seeds released Nov.

Distribution & Habitat

- Kawaka: from Mangonui to Rotorua in North Is., north-west Nelson area in South Is. Pahautea: mostly in wet, mountainous forests from Te Aroha south and lower levels on west coast of South Is.
- Kawaka: sea level to 600 m; pahautea: 250–1200 m.

▼ Pahautea foliage. (x2)

▼ Kawaka foliage. (x2)

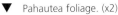

◄ A group of pahautea trees.

11 Kauri
Agathis australis

Appearance
- Young trees ('rickers') have tapering, narrow, conical forms. Mature: huge spreading crown on immense swollen branches.

- *Height:* up to 30 m.
- *Trunk:* up to 3 m through.
- *Bark:* young tree smoother; mature brown-ash grey, hammer marked, peels in thick flakes.

Foliage, Flowers & Fruit

- *Foliage:* juvenile leaves often bronze, 5–10 cm long by 5–12 mm wide, pointed, lanceolate, alternately arranged; adult greener, thick and leathery, blunt, short (only 2–3.5 cm long), sessile (no stalk), arranged either alternately or opposite.
- *Flowers:* male and female cones borne on same tree. Male cones cylindrical up to 5 cm long; female green, ovoid to 7.5 cm diameter.
- *Fruit:* after 25–30 years trees may begin to bear fertile seeds. Ripe female cones release brown, winged seeds.

Distribution & Habitat

- Lowland forests from Northland south to Tauranga.
- Sea level to 600 m.

▲ Mature female cones. (x0.5)

◀ Male cone and adult foilage. (approx x1)

◀ A kauri tree known as the McKinney Kauri, Parry Park near Warkworth (Dec 1977).

12 Tawa
Beilschmiedia tawa

Appearance
- A tall, erect tree with a spreading crown.
- *Height:* up to 25 m.
- *Trunk:* up to 1.2 m through, straight and smooth; develop stout, buttressed roots when old.
- *Bark:* grey; smooth, even-textured; older trees partially covered with light-coloured lichens and mosses.

Foliage, Flowers & Fruit
- *Foliage:* willow-like, aromatic leaves yellow-green above, paler bluish below; up to 10 cm long, 2 cm wide on slender petioles.

- *Flowers:* Sept; creamy green, borne on panicles up to 8 cm long, arising between axils of branchlets towards branch tip.
- *Fruit:* ripens Feb; dark purple; 2.5 cm oval drupes ('plums').

Distribution & Habitat
- Northern New Zealand, south to Clarence River and Westport in South Is.
- Sea level to 800 m.

▲ Mature foliage and flower panicles. (x0.5)

▶ Tawa drupes, March. (x2)

13 Taraire
Beilschmiedia tarairi

Appearance

- Juvenile trees slender with tall trunks and sparse, slim upright branches; mature tree has crown of stout, spreading branches.
- *Height:* up to 22 m.

- *Trunk:* up to 1 m across; straight, slender.
- *Bark:* dark brown but lichen growth gives light, grey-white appearance; smooth, hard.

Foliage, Flowers & Fruit

- *Foliage:* leaves bright green above with veins marked by reddish-brown tomentum (velvety covering), pale bluish green and dull below, midvein and main laterals raised and clad with tomentum; 15 cm long by 6 cm wide on petioles 1.5 cm long; elliptic to obovate-oblong in shape, arranged alternately. Leaf bases, petioles and flower stalks also clad with tomentum.

- *Flowers:* Sept–Dec; creamy tuft flowers on short axillary panicles.
- *Fruit:* ripens Apr–May; large, oval, dark purple drupe, 3.5 cm long.

Distribution & Habitat

- Lowland areas from North Cape to Raglan and Mt Hikurangi; common in kauri forests.
- Sea level to 350 m.

▼ Upper surface of leaves and spray of flowers, Dec. (x0.5)

▼ Taraire drupes, May. (x0.5)

14 Pigeonwood / Porokaiwhiri
Hedycarya arborea

Appearance

- A small, erect tree with ascending branches.
- *Height:* up to 12 m.
- *Trunk:* up to 50 cm through.
- *Bark:* mid-brown; fairly smooth; often partially covered with moss and lichen.

Foliage, Flowers & Fruit

- *Foliage:* leaves shining above, duller and paler below, with distinct venation; up to 12 cm long, 5 cm wide, on petioles 2 cm long; elliptic to obovate or lanceolate to oblanceolate in shape, with margins saw-toothed, serrate or plain.
- *Flowers:* male Oct, female Dec; light green; borne on many-flowered branching racemes; no sepals or petals but undifferentiated perianths of tepals; strongly

aromatic; male 1 cm across, female smaller.
- *Fruit:* female trees ripen Oct–Dec after 12 months; clusters of bright reddish-orange drupes, 1.5 cm long.

Distribution & Habitat
- In wet areas with rich soils, throughout North Is. south to Banks Peninsula; also Three Kings Is.
- Sea level to 800 m.

▲ Mature foliage and ripening drupes, Nov. (x0.5)

◄ A leaf undersurface.

15 Horopito / Pepper tree
Pseudowintera colorata

Appearance
- Most commonly a rounded shrub, with branches to ground level; tree is rounded, with upright spreading branches.
- *Height:* shrub 1–2.5 m; tree up to 10 m.

- *Trunk:* up to 1 m through.
- *Bark:* dark greenish-grey, often appearing black through fungus; smooth.

Foliage, Flowers & Fruit

- *Foliage:* leathery leaves are dull yellow-brown to green above, usually blotched and edged with red, bluish below with strong midvein; 2–8 cm long by 1–3 cm wide, on petioles 1 cm long, elliptic to obovate-elliptic in shape; aromatic when crushed. New shoots in spring brilliant red.
- *Flowers:* Sept–Dec; creamy yellow; arise singly or in clusters of up to 5 or more along stems; faintly aromatic.
- *Fruit:* berries ripen Mar–Apr; black, sometimes deep reddish-black; ovoid.

Distribution & Habitat

- Forests and forest margins and scrublands throughout most of New Zealand.
- Sea level to 1200 m.

◀ Leaf upper surface showing typical red edging and blotching. (x1)

◀ Typical bluish undersurface of leaf. (x1)

Mangeao
Litsea calicaris

Appearance
- Small, much-branched tree; spreading rounded crown in open; more confined and erect in forest.

- *Height:* up to 12 m.
- *Trunk:* up to 80 cm through.
- *Bark:* dark-brown; smooth; often lichen-covered.

Foliage, Flowers & Fruit

- *Foliage:* leathery leaves are dark glossy green above, duller and paler below; 5–12 cm long, up to 5 cm wide; ovate to ovate-ellliptic in shape.
- *Flowers:* Sept; male and female on separate trees; sweet-scented, greenish-yellow flowers borne profusely on umbels arising from axils towards branch tips.

- *Fruit:* ripens Feb; dark purple; 1.5–2 cm oval drupes sit on pedicel produced from the flower tube.

Distribution & Habitat

- Lowland forests from North Cape south to Mokau and East Cape.
- Sea level to 600 m.

▼ Drupes, Feb. (x0.5)

▼ Male flower shedding pollen, Sept. (x3)

▶ Mangeao flowers and foliage.

17 Pukatea
Laurelia novae-zelandiae

Appearance
- A tall tree with branches upright and fairly open.
- *Height:* up to 36 m.
- *Trunk:* up to 2 m through, clean and straight, prominently buttressed; free of branches for some distance from ground in forest, branches lower when exposed.
- *Bark:* pale brown; rather blistery.

Foliage, Flowers & Fruit

- *Foliage:* thick, leathery leaves are glossy above, less shining and paler below; up to 8 cm long, 5 cm wide, on petioles up to 1 cm long; elliptic to elliptic-obovate in shape, with margins coarsely and bluntly serrate.
- *Flowers:* Oct–Nov; flowers are perfect (bisexual) or modified perfect flowers with red stamens and yellow abortive staminodes; other male and female flowers on the same tree; all arise as axillary racemes up to 3 cm long with hairy peduncles.
- *Fruit:* ripens Mar; green turning brown; false fruits urn-shaped.

Distribution & Habitat

- Throughout New Zealand in swampy forests, damp gullies and creek beds.
- Sea level to 610 m.

▼ Male flowers with anthers but no stigma, Oct. (x1)

▼ Pukatea leaves. (x0.5)

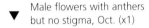

◀ Female flowers with staminodes and stigma but no stamens, Nov. (x4)

18 **Hutu**
Ascarina lucida

Appearance
- Small tree with erect, thin branchlets.
- *Height:* up to 8 m.
- *Bark:* pale; smooth.

Foliage, Flowers & Fruit
- *Foliage:* leathery leaves are bright green above, paler and less shining below with midveins strongly raised, tips dark coloured; up to

▲ Hutu trees.

2–8 cm long by 3.5 cm wide, on petioles up to 1 cm long; elliptic in shape, margins coarsely serrated with sharp, dark-coloured tips. Branchlets red.

Flowers: Sept; sexes on same or separate tree; flower spikes about 3.5 cm long at ends of branchlets; each spike has male flowers with 1 or rarely 2 stamens and female flowers which have a single carpel.

- *Fruit:* ripens Mar–Apr; pale blue-green, oval berries.

Distribution & Habitat
- Throughout New Zealand in forests, occasionally in North Is., more common on west coast of South and Stewart Is.
- Sea level to 760 m.

Hutu leaves, showing the coarsely serrated margins.

A typically pendulous spike of male flowers, Sept.

19 Mahoe / Whiteywood
Melicytus ramiflorus

Appearance
- Small tree with upright, usually spreading branches.
- *Height:* up to 10 m.
- *Trunk:* up to 60 cm through; usually short, branching starts close to ground. Branchlets brittle.
- *Bark:* whitish; smooth; usually covered with fine white lichens.

Foliage, Flowers & Fruit
- *Foliage:* young leaves bright yellow-green, mature are greener; 5–15 cm long, 3–5 cm wide.
- *Flowers:* Dec; profuse white flowers in clusters of 2–10 on slender pedicels up to 5 mm long arise in axils of leaves and along branchlets; unisexual, with males and females on separate trees; female smaller.
- *Fruit:* ripens Mar; round, dark purple berries borne profusely.

Distribution & Habitat

- One of commonest native trees throughout New Zealand in forests and scrublands, often predominant on partially cleared land.
- Sea level to 600 m.

▶ Ripe berries clothe the branchlets, Mar. (x1)

▼ Typical mahoe leaf upper surface. (approx x1)

▲ Male flowers, Dec. (x3)

20 Kotukutuku / Native fuchsia
Fuchsia excorticata

Appearance

- A shrub, or more usually a small tree with open, spreading branches.
- *Height:* up to 14 m. Largest fuchsia in world.
- *Trunk:* 60–80 cm through, in very old trees up to 1 m, with base gnarled and twisted.

- *Bark:* red; papery outer peeling to satiny-smooth, pale yellowish-brown or yellowish-green inner.

Foliage, Flowers & Fruit

- *Foliage:* leaves dark green above, pale and silvery below; up to 8 cm long, 4 cm wide, on petioles up to

4 cm long; ovate-lanceolate or ovate-oblong in shape. Deciduous.

• *Flowers:* Aug–Dec; opening flower is green shaded with purple, it turns purple then deep red; flowers hang downwards, each on a slender pedicel up to 15 mm long that arises from axil of a leaf or directly from a branch before leaves appear. Two forms: hermaphrodite with deep blue pollen; female with short stamens and a very long style; not on same tree.

• *Fruit:* ripens Dec–Mar; dark purple to almost black berries; narrow, about 1 cm long.

Distribution & Habitat

• Throughout New Zealand and at Auckland Is., in forests and scrublands. Common in second-growth areas and on stream banks.

• Sea level to 1060 m.

▼ Leaf upper surface. (x1)

▼ Hermaphrodite flowers, Nov. (x0.5)

21 Rewarewa / New Zealand honeysuckle
Knightia excelsa

Appearance

- A tall, pyramidal, upright-branching tree.
- *Height:* up to 30 m.
- *Trunk:* up to 1 m through; often 12–15 m before first branch arises.
- *Bark:* greyish; clean, finely textured.

Foliage, Flowers & Fruit

- *Foliage:* thick, leathery leaves are dark green above with distinct midvein, pale and browner below; up to 20 cm long, 2.5–4 mm wide; linear-oblong in shape, with acute tips and bluntly serrate margins. Young branchlets are angular and

covered with a dark brown tomentum along midvein and lower leaf surface.

- *Flowers:* Nov; deep red; inflorescence (the flower cluster) contains number of individual flowers, with spirally coiled perianth segments, crowded into raceme; arranged in axillary or terminal racemes, either in pairs or singly; objectionable smell.

- *Fruit:* ripens June after 12 months; orangey-brown, tomentose fruits up to 4 cm long; winged seeds.

Distribution & Habitat
- Throughout North Is. and Marlborough Sounds in South Is.
- Sea level to 850 m.

▼ Leaves of mature rewarewa.

▼ A flower cluster, Nov. (x0.3)

Tarata / Lemonwood
Pittosporum eugenioides

Appearance
- Juvenile: compact, pyramidal; when mature forms a rounded crown then becomes open, stoutly branched.

- *Height:* up to 12 m; the largest New Zealand pittosporum.
- *Trunk:* up to 60 cm through.
- *Bark:* greyish-white; rough.

Foliage, Flowers & Fruit

- *Foliage:* leaves are yellow-green above when juvenile, glossy green with yellow midvein when mature, paler and duller below; 10–15 cm long, 2–4 cm wide, on slender petioles up to 2 cm long; elliptic in shape, with undulating margins; strong lemon-like smell when crushed.
- *Flowers:* Oct–Dec; yellow flowers 1–1.5 cm across, in large terminal clusters with hairy peduncles; sweet, honey-like scent.
- *Fruit:* ripens Mar; green; small, egg-shaped, 2–3 valved capsule.

Distribution & Habitat

- Throughout New Zealand in forests, along forest margins and on stream banks.
- Sea level to 600 m.

▼ Flowers of tarata, Oct.

▼ The pale bark of a mature tree.

◀ Last season's ripe fruits on left; new season's green fruits on right (Mar).

23 Karo
Pittosporum crassifolium

Appearance

- Shrub or small tree with ascending branches.
- *Height:* up to 9 m.
- *Trunk:* up to 8 cm through.
- *Bark:* dark grey; smooth.

Foliage, Flowers & Fruit

- *Foliage:* thick, leathery leaves are glossy green above with distinct 'crackled' appearance, dense whitish tomentum on leaf undersides and stout petioles;

5–7 cm long by 2.5 cm wide; obovate-elliptic to narrow obovate or obovate-cuneate in shape, with rolled edges. Branchlets, peduncles also clothed with dense whitish or buff tomentum.

- *Flowers:* Sept; red to dark red; arise in terminal umbels of 3–10 flowers; unisexual; strongly scented.
- *Fruit:* ripens Apr–May; 3–4-valved seed capsules, up to 3 cm long, covered by a white or yellowish tomentum; shining black seeds on peduncles about 1.5 cm long are set in a golden-yellow mass of glutin.

Distribution & Habitat

- North Cape to Poverty Bay along streams and forest margins, mainly near coast. Now widely spread by cultivation.
- Sea level to 950 m.

▼ Leaf undersurface showing tomentum and rolled edges.

▼ A terminal umbel of karo flowers, Sept. (approx x1)

Kohuhu
Pittosporum tenuifolium

Appearance

- Small tree with spreading, erect branches. In forests, grows with a slender, straight trunk, elsewhere it forms a tight, much-branched tree from the ground upwards.
- *Height:* up to 9 m.
- *Trunk:* up to 15 cm through.
- *Bark:* grey; blistered when old.

Foliage, Flowers & Fruit

- *Foliage:* leaves glossy silvery green above, paler and hairless below; 3–7 cm long by 1–2 cm wide; oblong to oblong-ovate or elliptic-ovate in shape, with obtuse or acute tips and wavy margins. Branchlets glossy deep red or reddish-black.

- *Flowers:* Nov; reddish purple, turning black; occur singly or as small cymes in axils of leaves near branch tips; either male or female on separate trees or together on same tree, occasionally bisexual; scented at dusk.
- *Fruit:* ripens Apr–May; 3-valved

seed capsules; black seeds held in sticky yellow glutin.

Distribution & Habitat
- From near North Cape southwards; not found west of main divide in South Is.
- Sea level to 920 m.

▼   Leaf upper surface. (x1)

▲   Leaf lower surface. (x1)

▶   Flowers of kohuhu. (x1)

Pohutukawa
Metrosideros excelsa

Appearance

- Young tree bushy; mature tree has a broad crown of horizontally spreading branches, often twisted, bent or gnarled; often has aerial roots from low branches or trunk.
- *Height:* to 20 m.
- *Trunk:* short, thick; to 2 m through.
- *Bark:* grey; thick, stringy, peels in long, narrow flakes.

Foliage, Flowers & Fruit

- *Foliage:* leaves glossy green above; up to 10 cm long, 5 cm wide, on petioles 10–12 mm long in 4 rows on stem; elliptic in shape; mature thick and leathery, juvenile softer. Branchlets, petioles and leaf undersides covered by dense white tomentum.
- *Flowers:* Dec: hence 'New Zealand Christmas tree'; distinctive red

stamens in large spiky balls; flower clusters occur in pairs at tips of branchlets.

- *Fruit:* ripens Apr; seed capsules with reddish-brown seeds; mostly 4-valved.

Distribution & Habitat

- North of Kawhia and Opotiki along coasts; inland near Taupo and Rotorua lakes; also extensively planted in North Is., Nelson, Banks Peninsula south to Dunedin.
- Sea level to 350 m.

▲ Pohutukawa flower, Jan. (x0.25)

▶ Pohutukawa leaves showing upper and lower surfaces.

◀ Mature pohutukawa tree, Dec.

26 Rata and Southern rata
Metrosideros robusta and *M. umbellata*

Appearance

- Rata a tall tree, with often fused aerial roots, huge spreading branches. Begins as epiphyte perched on host tree, aerial roots grow downwards to ground, finally enclosing host. Southern rata grows from seed in ground; upright spreading branches.

- *Height:* to 25 m; Southern rata to 15 m.
- *Trunk:* to 2.5 cm through; Southern rata to 1 m.
- *Bark:* grey; thin, falls in small rectangular flakes; Southern rata thicker.

Foliage, Flowers & Fruit

- *Foliage:* rata's thick, leathery leaves are glossy green above, paler below; up to 5 cm long, 2 cm wide; elliptic, rounder and shorter than Southern rata and dotted with many oil glands.
- *Flowers:* Nov–Jan; similar to pohutukawa (No. 25) but smaller and usually more intense red. Southern rata flowers more brilliant red.
- *Fruit:* ripens Apr; similar to pohutukawa.

Distribution & Habitat

- Rata: throughout North Is., in South Island south to Westport. Southern rata: Whangarei south to Stewart Is. but rare in North Is; in higher rainfall regions.
- Sea level to 900 m.

▲ Rata flowers; Southern rata flowers are a more brilliant red. (x1)

▶ Southern rata leaf upper surface, with flower buds at the branchlet tip.

◀ A huge rata, Lake Waikaremoana.

27

Kanuka
Kunzea ericoides

Appearance

- Shrub of varying form or a spreading tree with ascending branches.
- *Height:* up to 15 m.
- *Trunk:* up to 25 cm through.
- *Bark:* grey; stringy, peeling in long flakes.

Foliage, Flowers & Fruit

- *Foliage:* aromatic leaves up to 12–15 mm long, 2 mm wide; linear to narrow-lanceolate in shape with acute tips; arise singly or in groups of 3–5.
- *Flowers:* summer; profuse small, white, fragrant flowers, about 5 mm across, arise as 2 or 5-flowered cymes.
- *Fruit:* ripens Jul, narrow, long, 5-valved seed capsules.

Distribution & Habitat

- Throughout North and South Is., in forests and scrubland.
- Sea level to 900 m.

Family MYRTACEAE
Genus *Kunzea*

▲ Branch showing leaves and flowers, Dec.

▲ Kanuka bark. Manuka (No. 28) is similar.

◀ Kanuka tree in full flower, Jan.

28

Manuka / Tea tree
Leptospermum scoparium

Appearance
- Shrub of varying form and habit or a tree with spreading ascending branches. Forms areas of scrub that protect regenerating forest seedlings.

- *Height:* up to 4 m.
- *Trunk:* up to 15 cm through.
- *Bark:* grey; stringy, peeling in long flakes.

Foliage, Flowers & Fruit

- *Foliage:* thick, leathery leaves are 4–12 mm long, up to 4 mm wide, narrowly lanceolate in shape; with prickly tip; undersides are dotted with aromatic glands. Branchlets and young leaves clothed with whitish silky hairs.
- *Flowers:* Sept–Feb; white (sometimes pink forms occur), arise singly in the axils of leaves; about 12 mm across; very profuse.
- *Fruit:* ripens Apr–May; hard, woody, broad, 5-valved seed capsules.

Distribution & Habitat

- Throughout New Zealand, including Chatham Is., in forests and scrubland.
- Sea level to 1000 m.

▲ LEFT: A branch showing manuka leaves.

▲ RIGHT: Flowers, Dec. (x2.5)

▶ Manuka seed capsules, July. Kanuka (No. 27) seed capsules are similar. (x2)

29

Ramarama
Lophomyrtus bullata

Appearance

- A shrub or small tree with thin, upright branches.
- *Height:* up to 6 m.
- *Trunk:* thin; up to 10 cm through.
- *Bark:* pale grey-green; smooth.

Foliage, Flowers & Fruit

- *Foliage:* thick, leathery leaves are blistered, and dark green with red blotches above (if tree is unshaded), pale below, with tomentum along midvein and

some side veins; up to 30 mm long, 15 mm wide, on petioles 2–5 mm long; broadly ovate in shape. Young stems and petioles are hairy.

- *Flowers:* Nov–Jan; white or very pale pink; arise singly on woolly peduncles in axils of leaves; sepals and petals dotted with very small glands and hairs.

- *Fruit:* ripens following Jan; dark red to black, ovoid berries.

Distribution & Habitat
- Throughout North Is., Nelson and Marlborough in open forests and along forest margins in coastal forests.
- Sea level to 600 m.

▼ Foliage showing the red-blistered leaves typical of a tree in the open, Oct.

▼ Foliage with berries, from a tree in the shade, June.

◀ A small ramarama tree.

30

Mountain ribbonwoods
Hoheria lyallii and *H. glabrata*

Appearance
- Small, spreading, deciduous trees.
- *Height:* up to 6 m. *H. glabrata* up to 10 m.
- *Trunk:* up to 12 cm through.
- *Bark:* grey-brown with distinctive white lichen; stippled.

Foliage, Flowers & Fruit
- *Foliage:* leaves light green above, paler below with prominent veins; 8 cm long by 5 cm wide; alternate, almost opposite. *H. glabrata* longer leaf petiole, branchlets less densely clothed with star-like hairs.
- *Flowers:* summer; white; about 4 cm across; flower stalks clothed with star-like hairs, denser in *H. lyalli*.
- *Fruit:* ripens Mar; wingless, 2-valved, single-seeded capsules.

Distribution & Habitat

- In mountains of South Is. on forest margins, stream terraces and shrubland. *H. lyallii* mainly on eastern side of main divide and *H. glabrata* on west side.
- 600–1050 m.

▲ Lower leaf surface of *H. lyalli*. (approx x0.75)

▲ Upper leaf surface of *H. glabrata*. (approx x0.75)

▶ Flower of *H. glabrata*. Those of *H. lyalli* are similar.

◀ A tree of *H. lyalli*.

31

Narrow-leaved lacebark
Hoheria angustifolia

Appearance

- Slender, upright-branched, spreading tree; juvenile bushy shrub with interlacing, flexible branchlets.
- *Height:* up to 10 m.
- *Trunk:* up to 24 cm through.
- *Bark:* greyish; smooth.

Foliage, Flowers & Fruit

- *Foliage:* leaves mid-green and shiny above, much paler below; juvenile up to 8 mm long, 7 mm wide on slender petioles 1–2 mm long; adult: up to 3 cm long, 1 cm wide; prominent serrations.
- *Flowers:* summer; smothered in white flowers; 5 styles to each flower; pedicels and sepals hairy.
- *Fruit:* ripens Mar; winged seeds.

Distribution & Habitat

- From Taranaki southwards through South Is. along forest margins; sometimes forming groves.
- Sea level to 900 m.

▼ Branchlet showing flowers, buds and leaf upper surfaces, Jan. (x0.8)

▲ Adult leaves showing the pale undersides. (x0.6)

▶ The smaller juvenile leaves. (approx x1)

32 Lacebark / Houhere
Hoheria populnea

Appearance
- Graceful, erect, much-branched, poplar-like tree.
- *Height:* up to 11 m.

- *Trunk:* up to 30 cm through.
- *Bark:* greyish-green; lace-like pattern.

Foliage, Flowers & Fruit

- *Foliage:* somewhat leathery leaves are shiny dark green above, with veins prominent, much paler below with raised veins; up to 14 cm long, 6 cm wide, on slender petioles up to 2 cm long; broad-ovate or ovate-lanceolate to elliptic in shape, with serrate margins; alternately arranged. Branchlets slender, clothed with a pale bark and grooved. Juveniles have entangled branchlets with leaves up to 3 cm long on delicate petioles up to 1 cm long; sometimes semi-deciduous.

- *Flowers:* Feb–Apr; smothered in white flowers, borne singly or in cymose clusters in leaf axils; 5 carpels; strong, sweet scent.
- *Fruit:* ripens following Dec; winged fruit with 5 seed cases, each with a single seed arranged as wings around a central axis.

Distribution & Habitat

- Naturally from North Cape to Waikato and Bay of Plenty. Now extensively in cultivation throughout New Zealand with many forms.
- Sea level to 450 m.

▼ Leaves with flower buds arising from the leaf axis.

▼ Houhere flower, Apr. There are five carpels. (x2)

33

Long-leaved lacebark / Houhere
Hoheria sexstylosa

Appearance
- Erect, much-branching, canopy tree; foliage tends to droop.
- *Height:* up to 6 m.

- *Trunk:* up to 25 cm through.
- *Bark:* greyish-green; lace-like pattern.

Foliage, Flowers & Fruit

- *Foliage:* somewhat leathery leaves are shiny dark green above, with veins prominent, much paler below with raised veins; up to 15 cm long and 5 cm wide; lanceolate in shape with very deeply serrate margins; alternately arranged; with dense clothing of star-like hairs on younger stems. Tiny leaves on juvenile plants.
- *Flowers:* Feb–Apr; smothered in white flowers; bisexual; borne singly or in cymose clusters in leaf axils; 6–7 carpels; strong, sweet scent.

- *Fruit:* ripens following Dec; winged fruit with 5 seed cases, each with a single seed arranged as wings around a central axis.

Distribution & Habitat

- From Whangarei south to Nelson, and from Banks Peninsula and near Gore; in forests and forest margins. Now extensively in cultivation throughout New Zealand.
- Sea level to 450 m.

▲ Flowers are produced in great abundance along the branchlets, Mar.

▲ Lower leaf surface. (x0.5)

34

Manatu / Ribbonwood
Plagianthus regius

Appearance

- Medium or large upright- and heavy-branched tree; bushy juvenile stage of tough, interlacing, springy branches.

- *Height:* up to 15 m.
- *Trunk:* up to 1 m through.
- *Bark:* grey; very rough, often discoloured by lichens and sooty fungus on older trees.

Foliage, Flowers & Fruit

- *Foliage:* soft leaves are dark green above, slightly paler below; up to 7.5 cm long, 5 cm wide, on petioles up to 3 cm long; vary from ovate to ovate-lanceolate or broadly ovate in shape, with acuminate tip and blunt marginal serrations; deciduous. Juvenile leaves small (to 20 cm long by 15 mm wide on petioles 5 mm long), broadly ovate, ovate-lanceolate or rounded, and irregularly lobed or crenate-serrate.
- *Flowers:* Oct–Jan; unisexual, males more yellowish than green, smaller females; abundant flowers only 3–4 mm across, on long, paniculate cymes hanging down from branches.
- *Fruit:* ripens Jan–Feb; reddish, ovoid, pointed fruit 3–5 mm long; sits in cup formed by sepals, with a seed in each carpel.

Distribution & Habitat

- From Mangonui south through North, South and Stewart Is. on riverbanks and alluvial terraces and along lowland forest margins.
- Sea level to 450 m.

▲ The bark of manatu.

► The long hanging cyme of male flowers, Oct.

35

Putaputaweta
Carpodetus serratus

Appearance

- Juvenile tree: zigzag, spreading, interlacing branchlets with much smaller leaves; adult: branches spread outward in flattened tiers.
- *Height:* up to 10 m.
- *Trunk:* up to 30 cm through.
- *Bark:* greyish-white and lichen covered; dimpled.

Foliage, Flowers & Fruit

- *Foliage:* thin but leathery leaves are glossy dark green and often mottled above, paler below with distinct venation, new leaves have reddish tinge; up to 6 cm long, 3 cm wide; ovate-elliptic to broad-elliptic in shape, with finely serrated margins.

- *Flowers:* Jan; white with yellow stamens; bisexual; 5 mm across, clustered on broad white panicles up to 5 cm across; sepals, petals and stamens attached to cup-like receptacle.
- *Fruit:* ripens Mar; panicles of round berries often with a prominent girdle above the middle, purple to black when fully ripe.

Distribution & Habitat
- Throughout New Zealand including Stewart Is. along forest margins and stream banks.
- Sea level to 1050 m.

▼ Leaf upper surface. (x1)

▼ Flowers, Dec. (x6)

▶ Panicles of ripening fruits, Mar.

◀ Putaputaweta in flower, Dec.

36

Maire tawaki
Syzygium maire

Appearance
- Many-branched tree forming a spreading canopy.
- *Height:* up to 15 m.
- *Trunk:* up to 60 cm through.
- *Bark:* grey; smooth.

Foliage, Flowers & Fruit
- *Foliage:* leaves dark green above and below, often marked by small blisters and dark patches, new shoots olive-green; about 4 cm long by 1.5 cm wide, on slender

petioles 8–10 mm long; tapering at each end, with wavy margins; arise oppositely in pairs; branchlets 4-angled.

- *Flowers:* Mar; about 12 mm across, with small pink petals, green sepals; arise in clusters on single stalks, borne in many-flowered cymes.
- *Fruit:* ripens following Mar;

bunches of brilliant red, ovoid berries about 12 mm across; each hold 1 seed.

Distribution & Habitat

- Throughout North Is. in lowland swampy and boggy forests, and in northern tip of South Is.
- Sea level to 450 m.

▼ Young shoot showing upper and lower leaf surfaces. (x1)

▼ Flower, Mar. (x1)

▶ The berries each hold one seed. (x1.75)

37

Whau
Entelea arborescens

Appearance
- Upright spreading tree forming a canopy, also grows as a shrub.
- *Height:* up to 6 m.
- *Trunk:* up to 25 cm through.
- *Bark:* brown-green; soft, wrinkled and pustulate (blistered).

Foliage, Flowers & Fruit
- *Foliage:* drooping, soft leaves are bright green above, paler below with raised venation; 15–25 cm long by 15–20 cm wide (up to 60 cm long in off-shore islands) on long petioles; serrated margins. Branchlets and young leaves clothed with soft, branched hairs.

- *Flowers:* Nov; large white flowers about 2.5 cm across, with crinkled petals, arise in large, flat clusters from leaf axils towards tips of branchlets.
- *Fruit:* ripens Feb; reddish-brown; distinctive large capsule covered with spines like bidibid burrs, occur in clusters upright above the leaves at the branch tips.

Distribution & Habitat
- From North Cape south to Mokau River mouth and Bay of Plenty, then spasmodically to Nelson/Marlborough, in coastal and lowland forests.
- Sea level to 250 m.

▼ Leaf upper surface. (x0.25)

▼ Leaf lower surface. (x0.25)

▶ Whau flowers, Nov. (approx x1)

◀ A whau growing out from a cliff, Dec.

38

Wineberry / Makomako
Aristotelia serrata

Appearance

- Small, upright spreading tree, many branched; forms dense thickets in clearings after slips or felling; tall, slender form on roadsides.

- *Height:* up to 10 m.
- *Trunk:* up to 30 cm through.
- *Bark:* young bark red, old black; crinkled.

Foliage, Flowers & Fruit

- *Foliage:* membranous, translucent leaves are light green above, paler and often reddish below, veins prominent; up to 12 cm long, 8 cm wide, on slender petioles up to 5 cm long; oppositely arranged; deeply serrated margins; shapes can vary on same tree; deciduous in colder areas.
- *Flowers*: Nov; borne on panicles up to 10 cm long; male and female on separate trees, male are pale and darken with age, female without stamens; colour varies between trees.
- *Fruit:* ripens Mar; panicles of deep red to almost black berries, about 5 mm across.

Distribution & Habitat

- Throughout New Zealand in forests and scrubland, along forest margins and roadsides.
- Sea level to 1050 m.

▲ Panicles of ripe berries, Mar. (approx x1)

▶ Leaf upper surface. (x0.75)

◀ A wineberry tree in the forest.

39

Hinau
Elaeocarpus dentatus

Appearance
- Upright branching forming a canopy tree; distinctive juvenile stage of narrow leaves.
- *Height:* up to 18 m.
- *Trunk:* up to 1 m through.
- *Bark:* greyish; becomes rough with age.

Foliage, Flowers & Fruit
- *Foliage:* leaves light green above, paler below; about 12 cm long, 2–3 cm wide, on stout petioles 25 mm long borne at tips of branchlets; small pits (domatia) visible on lower surface. Juvenile stage leaves are narrow, 10–15 cm long with wavy margins.

- *Flowers:* Oct–Dec; white; borne on silky-hairy peduncle; droop from long racemes arising from leaf axils or direct from branches.
- *Fruit:* ripens May; purple, ovoid drupe up to 18 mm long.

Distribution & Habitat

- Throughout North and South Islands in lowland forests.
- Sea level to 600 m.

▼ Hinau flowers droop from long racemes, Nov. (x2)

▼ Leaf upper surface. (x1)

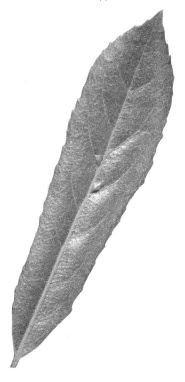

◀ Hinau trees in full flower, Dec.

40 Kamahi and Tawhero/towhai
Weinmannia racemosa and *W. silvicola*

Appearance

- Kamahi: spreading tree. Tawhero: canopy-forming, but many are erect with ascending branches.
- *Height:* to 25 m; tawhero to 15 m.
- *Trunk:* to 1.2 m through, tawhero to 1 m.
- *Bark:* greyish, blotched with white; quite smooth.

Foliage, Flowers & Fruit

- *Foliage:* thick, leathery leaves of adult kamahi are shiny dark green above, pale below with prominent veins, young new leaves reddish; 3–10 cm long, 2–4 cm wide; opposite; elliptic to broad ovate, with bluntly serrate margins. Tawhero: 4–7 cm long, 2–3 cm

wide; compound; elliptic to obovate-oblong.

- *Flowers:* Nov–Mar; white stamens with red stalks and pedicels; both trees produce racemes (up to 12 cm long) of flowers in profusion.
- *Fruit:* ripens Mar; reddish, 2–3-valved seed capsule.

Distribution & Habitat

- Kamahi: Auckland to Stewart Is. in lowland forests. Tawhero: from Mangonui to Waikato and Bay of Plenty in lowland forests and along forest margins.
- Sea level to 900 m.

▼ Spray of kamahi leaves.

▼ Spray of tawhero leaves.

▶ Tawhero flowers, Jan. (x0.5)

◀ A kamahi tree starting to flower, Dec.

41 Tawari
Ixerba brexioides

Appearance
- Bushy or canopy tree, with upright branches.

- *Height:* up to 15 m.
- *Trunk:* up to 60 cm across.
- *Bark:* grey; flaking

Foliage, Flowers & Fruit

- *Foliage:* thick, leathery leaves are glossy green above, paler below with distinct midvein; narrow, up to 16 cm long, 4 cm wide; margins have widely separated blunt teeth, each tipped with a gland.
- *Flowers:* Dec; conspicuous creamy-white flowers 2.5–3.5 cm across, borne on panicles at tips of branchlets; the 5 stamens stand erect from 5 petals; bisexual.

- *Fruit:* ripens Apr–May; seed capsules split into 5 valves, 2 black seeds in each valve.

Distribution & Habitat

- In North Is. from about Cape Brett to Ureweras in dark shady places in hilly and mountain forest interiors.
- Sea level to 900 m.

▼ Leaf undersurfaces showing blunt teeth. (x0.5)

▼ Flower, Dec. (x2)

Kowhai
Sophora tetraptera and *S. microphylla*

Appearance

- *S. tetraptera* a small, spreading tree; no juvenile form. *S. microphylla* smaller, more feathery looking, branches more spreading and drooping; juvenile a twiggy shrub with yellow, flexible, interlacing branchlets; adult branches more spreading and drooping. Two varieties are recognised: *fulvida* and *longicarinata*.

- *Height:* to 12 m; *S. microphylla* to 10 m.
- *Trunk:* to 60 cm through.
- *Bark:* greyish-brown; furrowed with age.

Foliage, Flowers & Fruit

- *Foliage: S. tetraptera* leaves are feathery, mid-green, up to 15 cm long, pinnately compound with 10–20 pairs of leaflets 15–35 mm

long; ovate to elliptic-oblong; clad with appressed silky hairs. Branchlets clothed with pale-brownish tomentum when young, but lack hairs when mature. *S. microphylla* leaves 15 cm long, with 20–40 pairs of obovate-oblong

leaflets, each 5–7 mm long on short petioles; hairy leaflets and rachis covered with dense golden-brown tomentum.

- *Flowers: S. tetraptera* Sept/Oct; yellow to golden yellow; each about 5 cm long, with 5 unequal

▼   Leaves of *S. tetraptera* each have 10–20 pairs of leaflets.

▼   Leaves of *S. microphylla* each have 20–40 pairs of leaflets.

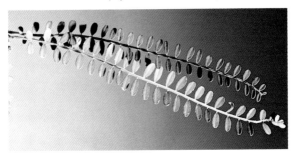

◄   *Sophora tetraptera* in flower, Oct.

petals, in 4–10-flowered racemes; raceme stalks, calyx and flower pedicels clothed with silky-brown tomentum. *S. microphylla* similar.

- *Fruit:* both species ripens Jul; seed pods up to 20 cm long with 6 or more seeds, yellow turning brown.

Distribution & Habitat

- *S. tetraptera* in North Is. from East Cape to Ruahine Range; *S. microphylla* in North, South and Chatham Is; growing wild along streams and forest margins; one of the most common natives, now widespread through cultivation.
- Sea level to 450 m.

▼ Flowers of *S. tetraptera* showing the long keel, shorter wings and even shorter standard, Sept. (approx x1)

▼ Flowers of *S. microphylla* with the wing and standard of equal length and the keel only slightly longer than the standard, Oct. (approx x1)

Glossary

acuminate: tapering to a fine point

alternate: arising singly along an axis

anther: the pollen-bearing part of a stamen

appressed: closely and flatly pressed against a surface

aril: accessory seed covering, usually pulpy

ascending: growing upwards, usually at a narrow angle from the vertical

axil: the upper angle between two dissimilar parts

axillary: placed in the axil of a leaf

berry: a fleshy fruit containing a number of seeds but not a 'stone'

bloom: a white powdery cladding

calyx: the outer, usually greenish-coloured whorl of parts in a flower

capsule: a dry fruit that splits open to release its seeds

carpel: the female unit of a flower consisting of the ovary, style and stigma

catkin: a spike-like inflorescence with unisexual flowers

compound: formed of several similar parts

compressed: flattened

cone: the fruiting parts of a conifer

crenate: with shallow, rounded teeth

cuneate: wedge-shaped

cyme: an inflorescence, usually symmetrical, with the oldest flowers innermost (adj. cymous)

deciduous: losing its leaves in the autumn

domatia: small pits on the lower surface of a leaf or between the mid and lateral veins

drupe: a fruit with a 'stone' or seed surrounded by a fleshy layer

fruit: the ripened ovary containing the seeds

inflorescence: a general term for the flowering parts

keel: a sharp central ridge

lanceolate: lance-shaped

leaflet: one element of a compound leaf

linear: very narrow with parallel margins

opposite: (of leaves) with a pair arising at the same level on opposite sides of the stem

ovate: (of leaves) egg-shaped, and attached by the broader end

ovoid: egg-shaped

ovule: the young seed within the ovary

panicle: branched, indeterminate inflorescence

pedicel: the stalk of an individual flower

peduncle: a stalk bearing one or many flowers

perianth: the sepals and petals of a flower taken together

petiole: the stalk of a leaf

phylloclade: a flattened stem which functions as a leaf

pinnate: compound with the parts arranged on either side of the axis

raceme: an unbranched indeterminate inflorescence

rachis (rhachis): the axis of an inflorescence or of a compound leaf

receptacle: the expanded apical portion of the stalk on which the flower is borne

scale: a minute, leaf-like structure, usually dry and membraneous

serrate: sharply toothed

sessile: without any stalk

spike: an unbranched, indeterminate, elongate inflorescence with sessile flowers

stamen: the male organ of a flower

stoma: a pore in the leaf epidermis through which gases pass (pl. stomata)

tepal: an individual member of the perianth of a flower

tomentum: a dense covering of more or less matted, appressed, soft hairs (adj. tomentose)

umbel: a more or less umbrella-shaped inflorescence with its pedicels arising from a common centre

vein: a strand of conducting and usually strengthening tissue in a leaf

venation: the arrangement of the veins in a leaf

whorl: an arrangement of three or more parts at the same level around an axis

Index of common names

Index of scientific names